MW01225546

Summit 21

Summit 21

Ashley Evans

RESOURCE *Publications* · Eugene, Oregon

SUMMIT 21

Copyright © 2022 Ashley Evans. All rights reserved. Except for
brief quotations in critical publications or reviews, no part of this
book may be reproduced in any manner without prior written
permission from the publisher. Write: Permissions, Wipf and Stock
Publishers, 199 W. 8th Ave., Suite 3, Eugene, OR 97401.

Resource Publications
An Imprint of Wipf and Stock Publishers
199 W. 8th Ave., Suite 3
Eugene, OR 97401

www.wipfandstock.com

PAPERBACK ISBN: 978-1-6667-4676-1
HARDCOVER ISBN: 978-1-6667-4677-8
EBOOK ISBN: 978-1-6667-4678-5

08/30/22

For You,
A love eternal.

Disclaimer

Although this collection of poetry is based on true events, it reflects the author's present recollections of those experiences over time and does not claim to represent the experiences of others. Many characteristics, locations, and dates have been changed, events altered, and dialogue recreated. Some events presented are done so in allegory and metaphors and are fiction.

This book speaks of mental illness, abuse, suicide, alcohol, and drug use. If these words bring forth overwhelming feelings, please place the book down, rest, and reach out for support.

If you need support, please connect.

Canada
Talk Suicide Canada 1–833-456–4566
Mental Health Crisis Line 1-866-585-0445
Crisis Text Line 686868 (youth); 741741 (adult)

United States
United States National Suicide & Crisis Hotline 988
Substance Abuse and Mental Health Services Administration 1-800-662-4357
Crisis Text Line 741741

Contents

The Peak | 1

The Ridge | 65

The Summit | 137

The Descent | 161

The Peak

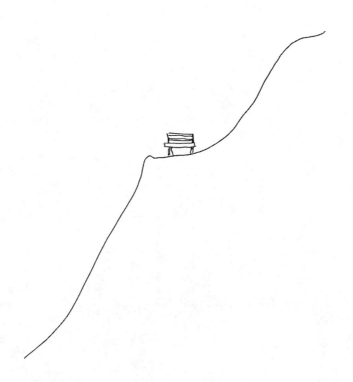

It began between prose—
yours, and then mine.
Your words cradled me,
like the arms I had
craved since leaving
the warm womb
of my mother.

You picked my strings like you had played me all your life—
I held the soulful lyrics to your dark melody.

No song had enough chords,
no hour enough minutes,
to fill my weary soul
in the ways that you did.

It was a cold, wet afternoon,
the day I saw your piercing green eyes
for the first time.

The gravel in my ears like
corn flakes on a Saturday morning.
The clouds gray,
angry,
sullen,
hung overhead.

    —*You were the sunshine.*

Seeing you for the first time
was the meeting of a lost
glance from years—
lifetimes—
before this one.
A reckoning.

    —We meet again my precious beloved.

You were draped in black
like the depth in your eyes.
I saw the darkness then
but tried to mask it
as pain.

Although, that is what darkness is—
darkness is bred from pain.

—*Hold that thought.*

I was timid in my green suede hiking boots.
Though not in the forest, this was the start
of a new quest for the summit.

—*The start of our adventure.*

I passed you a warm cappuccino,
and I shall always want to remember
seeing your hands for the first time as you reached out for it.

—*The scar on the left side of your right index finger
would become my home.*

Three days passed.

"I'm going to kiss you now,"
you said with a grin
as we sat face-to-face
on my white rawhide couch.

The sunlight trickled
through the translucent curtain.

The smell of espresso and lavender
hung in the air—
and you—soft, gentle.

 —I knew I wanted to kiss these lips forever.

Two wounded souls
had found each other.

Where there was once war,
we found peace.

You were the bunker,
I was the tent.
We took refuge in each other,
set up camp,
refuelled.

Laid bare in the open
sunshine of each other's hearts,
sang each other to sleep
in notes only we could hear.

—*You were my melody.*

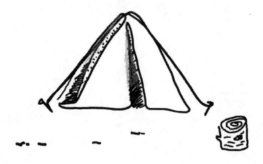

You reminded me
how it felt to be loved.
That my brokenness
had a place in this world.

I did not need to hide behind
a smiling complexion,
but rather,
you would hold my broken parts and celebrate them.

You found peace for your own brokenness
in mine.

Together we fit like an old
knit sweater.
Frayed and pilled, but home.

We moved quietly
as we built our love story.
For love stories can be quick,
or slow.
Ours was both—
quick to start,
slow to burn.

    —These are the best fires.

You released tears
like the spray of a great blue whale—
powerful and lasting,
as you recounted your life.

I held you as tightly
as the sky cradles the moon.

Each night I longed for your
peridot eyes
and scarred hands.

You opened me
in ways I had never been.

I would like to always remember
the way I looked at you
in the beginning—
a baby calf
seeing daylight for the first time.

You stroked my hair

while we listened to lyrics.

We found peace in the rhythmic verses that had once rattled
our broken hearts,

as we laid together and cried.

    —We had found companionship in our tears.

You touched the shallows of my veins,
the thorough of my brain,
you had a proficiency—
an artistry—
to the way you loved.

You started here,
my broken heart,
my fractured soul.
You held me here the longest.
Brought my memories warm almond milk, honey, and nutmeg,
wrapped a blanket around my troubled spirit,
and kissed my furrowed brow and weary words with lips
dripping with intent.

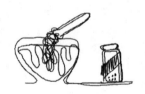

It took time,
but like seeds grow and bloom each year
you planted something inside of me.
I blossomed.
I learned how to breathe,
how to rest.
You held me
while I held grief
for those before you who still held pieces
of my heart.
You held me
as I cried,
when I was overcome with rainstorms,
when I was held hostage by fear,
you held me.

I learned how to trust again,
little by little,
day by day,
I learned how to feel safe again.
Each time you did not leave,
Every time you stayed,
my breath slowed.
My heart had caught its rhythm,
and I felt loved—
as deep and vast as the ocean,
as warm as metal on a sweltering day—
piercing,
burning.

So, we came together and shared old songs,
lyrics that tore us open,
and planted beliefs—
dreams—
questions—
inside of us.
The lyrics imagery
for what we held in our hearts.

Like bright city lights
in a wide-angle exposure,
we shone fluorescent—
our love blossomed electric.

It was a sunny afternoon.
Tuesday.
You in your worn-out black jeans,
pink and orange quarter-sleeve.
It was messy—
innocent—
vulnerable.
Come with me,
take my hand,
let me shelter you.

February 4th

Deliberating the menu at my kitchen island,
I wrote down our order in black cursive on a torn piece of
paper.

You asked me to call in the order
and for six and a half years I did.

We brought *us* out in public for the first time,
quietly driving through the darkness,
hands clasped together on the gear shift.

We would return five years later the night
you asked me to be yours forever.

 —*Sashimi and monkey brains.*

We moved from our matrimonial houses
on the seventeenth of April.
You packed me up in the back seat of your red, soft-top cabrio,
we held hands in an empty house,
on my old, white Italian leather couch.

You were everything to me—
you breathed life back into me,
brought sunshine where there were only clouds,
showered rain where there was drought,
you gave me hope.

　　—*But most of all, you taught me to trust in love again.*

Loving you was the easiest thing
I have ever done.

That spring saw red sunsets after days spent with sand between
our toes.

Your arms sat tightly around my waist,
as the soft of my head rested against your chest.
White twinkle lights scattered at our feet,
acoustic guitar and words on prose,
as we danced between the moonlight in the harbor
and the music on the sticky July air.

Manitou

We stepped one,
two,
three thousand steps
to the top.

Much like this
love of ours—
one step,
seven steps,
stop.
Breathe.
Water.
Sixty-nine steps—
stop,
kiss.

I had hoped our celebration at the top
would be not after three thousand steps
but after long lives well lived,
together.

Lentil stew with root broth,
roasted turnips and secret gravy,
chocolate almond cake.

You loved to be served,
and I loved to serve you.

Our families together grew
and for the first time in my life,
felt
complete.

We made big, elaborate plans.
Marriage,
babies,
houses,
travelling,
everything—
all things.

Our lives
delicately intertwined
and woven
into one beautiful,
deliberate,
existence
together.

Showering each other in love—
trips abroad and
the gentle drumming of local concerts.
Theater and
oysters,
pink sparkling wine and
overnight hikes to the most incredible summits.
Clear lakes and
quiet rocky beaches,
creamy orange tea and
candlelit dinners by the pier.
Dancing in the harbor under moonlight.

Was it all too much—
Was it not real life—

   —*I want you in real life. raw. messy. here. now.*

Together we fit like old
leather chaps on a cowboy
who had been riding
forty years.

Your laugh lines became
my entire existence,
imprinted in my memory—
a fossil, holding space for an eternity.
Our hands slid together
with the ease of
starting up a brand
new engine—
smooth,
exciting,
powerful.

   —*I will never tire of holding your hands.*

The twenty-first of September
we stood in the warm ocean—
you pulled me close
and we kissed
as the waves crashed against us.

    —A metaphor for our life to come.

January 1st

We moved in together.
The first house
that ever felt like home.

    —Sometimes home is a person.

March 21st

We told everyone it happened on Saint Valentines.

Wildberry mousse after a warm bike ride with yellow tulips in my basket,

the one you bought me at the Sunday market.

You laid a blanket on the sandy beach where we first met, and, bodies entangled, we watched the stars fill the sky overhead.

You asked me to be your wife—

every decision before, a precursor to that defining moment.

I had never been more sure of anything.

Yes.

—I would like to remind you of the beauty in that moment.

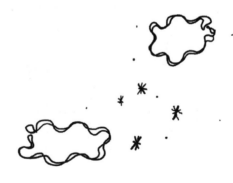

The rest of our lives had gained permission to start
as we stood hand-in-hand
watching the waves pound against the shore,
sand in-between our toes,
moon at our backs.

Our tomorrows were but a mystery,
our presence was all we had,
and that day was one of my favorites.

But even within this beauty sat a girl
who did not know how to love,
or how to let love in.

For four years I floundered
and pushed you away
when things felt too hard.

  —I would like to say I am sorry for that.

Through it all,

you always felt ten steps ahead of me.

I tried to catch up

but got tripped up on the meaning of forever.

I had learned that love was conditional,
given when I was good, withheld when I was bad.
Love was a hard concept to grasp,
and comfort harder still.

I had learned to protect myself, to keep a two-arms distance
from those I loved.
Those capable of hurting me.
I lost many friends and lovers this way.

The elusive goal was love; always love.
I watched helplessly as those I loved walked in and out of my life,
my heart Terminal One at Grand Central Station.

When years of abandonment—real or perceived—
and unrequited love
course through your veins,
fear starts calling the shots.

Fear is not easy to quiet.

It is the loudmouth in class who refuses to raise their hand.

Fear was my constant need for your validation, approval, and reassurance.

Pushing you further away when I needed you close.

I know now that vulnerability is the intersection where we would need to meet

to share in our fears and foster connection.

—You taught me this.

However, many nights I met the moonlight alone,
or filled our time with intrusive thoughts and worries,
our space becoming my own
and you graciously allowing it.

Silently, you assumed the weight of what felt like the world,
accepting the role you believed you must play,
and in my ignorance, I failed to notice your knees buckling.

We continued to walk in love.
Planning wedding dates
and building sandcastles with the kids.

Our days filled with laughter and hugs.

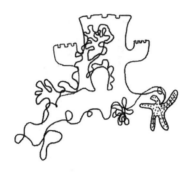

—*And small disagreements.*

Sideways words and glances that grew—
and grew—
what was once a molehill
became the mountain
we found ourselves at the bottom of.

—Our love, elusively at the top with no gardeners.

Love was a petroglyph Rubik's cube.
I did not know how to tend to the garden,
much less, how to live in it.
My weeds quietly suffocating the flowers you planted.

When fear crept in, I would disappear.
Books, silence, solitude.

But you always found me,
and held me.

—*Hold me just a little while longer.*

It took me longer
to catch up with you,
to learn about love,
to feel safety,
to meet you where you were.
Ready to love,
ready to be open.
I was the lotus,
rising from the muddy waters,
you were the lily pad,
face to the sun.

It took over one year
before I had even cried in front of you,
my emotions had been turned off—
a faucet run dry.

But with gentle care,
and just the right amount of pressure,
you opened me up.

I learned how to breathe in the arms of my sunshine,
how to relax against the small of your back.
The smell of your skin was my sanctuary,
your hands, my home.

I had finally found safety.
My forever,
where I belonged.

The word family made sense—
you were it—
you were it all—
everything.

You held us all together with your wide toothy grin and those deep peridot eyes,
and I loved you more deeply than you would ever come to realize.

Because when I finally blossomed into our love,
you were gone.
The knocking on my door had stopped,
silent refuge turned to silent war.
You no longer wanted in,
you wanted out.

I was too late.

I remember Old Orchard

A June afternoon hot enough to fry eggs on the sidewalk.
The still water lapped around your lime green bottoms
as you splashed around with my babies.
Your arms wrapped around me like you did not know how
to let go.

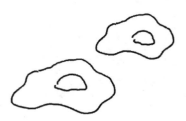

Chandler Oaks

The daisies were in full bloom for our June wedding.
We had fallen in love with the garden and blue shiplap walls,
and the grass tickled our ears as we gazed up to the sun and
agreed to promise our forever here.

Shallow Bay

Out on the gray igneous rock surrounded by crashing waves
you pointed at letter stamp spotted crabs
as my babies hung on your shoulders,
like your arms were the only safety they knew.
I watched you and knew,
you were our forever.

I remember 1496 Hickory Hill

and the look you gave me
while picking me up for my birthday dinner.
I was draped in a long eggplant skirt and a tasseled shawl
the colour of a cotton candy sunset,
your jaw was on the driveway you were walking on.

We listened to live music in the harbor, and you held me
as we mouthed the words to hallelujah.

And 267 Upper Crest

The sun was high that warm summer day.
I brought you cinnamon toothpaste and a blue toothbrush,
we made love on your old black and white cross-knit blan-
ket in the corner of an empty gray room.
You picked me up in the driveway as I left,
wrapped my legs around your waist
and kissed me.

    —Our first kiss outside for the world to see.

I remember feeling safety,
we were impenetrable.
I had found my forever in your love for me,
I believed in you deeper than I had believed in anything.

No matter the summit,
we would reach it.

The Ridge

Slowly,
then all at once,
the life we had
so meticulously built
began to unravel
like the thread of your mitten last December,
until there was only thread
and no knitting needle.

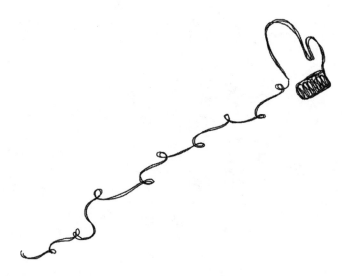

With no instructions,
and no needle,
how do we reknit?

    — With careful attention.

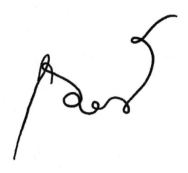

Slowly our life began to twist,
to contort in ways
I did not recognize.

It was unfamiliar,
confusion clouded my thoughts,
I did not understand what was happening to us.

   —*and I tried.*

Had I known then what I know now,
that rainy Tuesday may have ended much differently.

   —*You may have come home to me.*

It began one unseasonably warm October evening
after a mundane disagreement about a shirt.

The closing back door became an all too familiar sight,
nights of unanswered calls and texts,
and *you*—gone.

It felt easy then to place blame,
your empty side of our bed slow roasted balsamic beets for
my wounds and insecurities.

Unable to make sense of it,
I went to Pavone Bay and stayed with my mother.
We did not live together again after that.

    —*Trauma lives here.*

Seven nights my babies and I crammed on to a single foam
mattress tucked in the farthest corner of the room.
Seven nights I lay lost in a sea of worry and grief,
unsure of what I would come home to.
If there was a home to go back to.

But we found connection in lyrics and words on prose,
over shared experiences,
understanding,
and love.
Stronger than ever.

  —*Oh, how many times I have thought this and been wrong.*

You pealed open like an artichoke and shared with me your darkest parts,
the trauma and chains that kept your heart bound,
misplaced anger for those who were meant to love you.

—*Let me love you harder.*

Fourteen sleeps later I waited for your return.

I laid the kids to bed and prepared your peppermint tea in the green and white mug we bought you last December.

Bob Dylan played quietly as I thumbed through pages of The Alchemist on the pilled blue tweed couch—

the one we bought two months in.

I waited,

as time mocked me.

Then one word—

"Help."

Though not as intended,
we both died that night.

Do not hate me
you whispered,
as you lay shaking in my sweet Pele car,
now splattered with vodka, vomit, and our innocence.

How could you do this to me?
you screamed as the ambulance pulled up—
the phone caught the silence of a deafening cave,
1,000 metres underground,
as I caught my reflection in the black framed mirror—
empty eyes staring back.

You did not arrive there alone.

Together, our histories of trauma and abuse weaved a storm we could not weather—

although we tried.

Unresolved pain lying dormant within our cells awoke and broke loose that night.

The next morning I scrubbed that car clean in our driveway—
vomit laced water streaming on to the street,
an empty two-six in the recycling bin,
hot sun piercing my shoulders.

I ran 10k that afternoon and cried
as I circled Bulthame Road
and the place where you slept when you were not in our bed.

How did I not know
how low we had gotten?

   —*Questions I still ask myself.*

If only I had known.

   —*Statements I say to myself.*

I did not want to lose you.

   —*Truths.*

I did not want our scions to lose you.

   —*Truths.*

The bids killed something inside of me.

   —*My ability to breathe.*

Broken promises became the only promise worth believing,
I never knew if today
would be the last time I would hear the gentle roar of your
voice,
or tomorrow.
Bottled up grief surged
through my body day and night,
as I yearned to be with you,
wherever you were.

    —And, it broke me.

Venice Oak Resort

We met here the first time—
that third weekend in October.
We sat by the black slate fireplace,
and, weathered and worn, we drank ginger tea with forced smiles
as we watched a couple exchange vows in the banquet room across the hall.
Heartbreaking,
yet heartwarming at the same time—
processing grief I thought we were at the end of.

 —*It was only the beginning.*

I missed the you that I remembered,
I mourned you.
I did not know the moody eyes staring back at me,
pupils the end of a pin needle on the back of my neck.

A diagnosis had sat on the table,
doctors on each end,
but as the name was dropped,
time stopped.

Your chair spinning as the glass door shuttered,
silence.

They attached paper clips to their notes as the turquoise chair spun out into the marigold drywall.

    —And you were gone.

Wrapped in our itchy mauve wool blanket, I typed out the pages of old books you would read to me as I fell asleep each night.

I prayed the words would find you and remind you of the love you were surrounded by,

desperate to bring you home.

Words brimming with love and hope

pinged in a torn paper bag lying in the churchyard.

Three hours later.

The sound of wood chips under foot,
your gentle rap at the front door,
my cheek in a puddle of tears on the floor.

"Stop!"

The screaming echoed in my ears as if we were in the
Northern mountains,
the pounding in my chest the Grand Canyon.
They have you surrounded now—
heat to your face as they scream get down—
black enveloping the space all around.

All I wanted was to be able to hold you,
to tell you that I loved you.
I felt the pounding of your heart in my chest,
against the wood planked floors,
your sweat on my palms,
your tongue dry within my mouth.
I wanted to stroke your hair and tell you I loved you—
hold you and tell you it would all be okay.

But it was not.

Locked in an empty room,

you laid on a single strip of mattress, tears reflecting off the white fluorescent lights overhead.

I crawled into our bed with my babies,

our tears together filling the Pacific Ocean.

That was the night I lost my home.

—You.

Pale green walls and orange arrows became permanently etched in the cavities of my memory.

Tears streamed down my cheeks as I passed your black backpack to the nurse.

My eyes held to the ground as I prayed our family photos, and a hastily scribbled note would hold you in the same ways I yearned to.

> —*You were not broken, and we would make it through this.*

Mount Wilbur

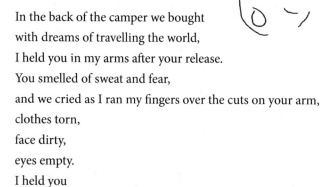

In the back of the camper we bought
with dreams of travelling the world,
I held you in my arms after your release.
You smelled of sweat and fear,
and we cried as I ran my fingers over the cuts on your arm,
clothes torn,
face dirty,
eyes empty.
I held you
in fear
as your tears seeped into my shoulder.

> —*I love you. More than there are words to say. Your tears
> are my own.*

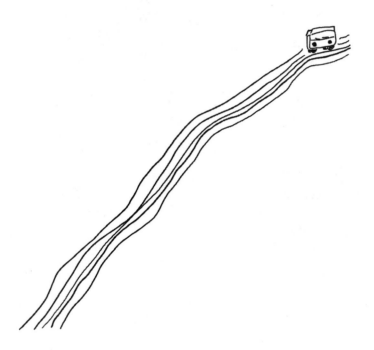

I held on to hope.

How could we be too far down the tracks to go back?
Had the tracks broken and splintered?
With some repair,
they could be better than new.
With tender care and attention,
the proper tools,
the time,
we could hop the train back—
back to when we held hands freely—
when you held my waist and looked
into my eyes as you proclaimed your love for me,
when we listened to music down in the harbor,
ate oysters around the corner,
drank cappuccinos at the beach—
two sugars, one cream.

   —*Back to when you were mine.*

Back to when I woke up beside you,
your freckled back soft as I lay nuzzled against it.
When you air-dried on our bed,
laying quietly as you stared at the white
checked roof overhead.
Back to when we sat together and ate dinner
as a family.
When we played board games,
and took baths on Saturdays.

The track was not broken—
the train crashed.
Debris filled the air as I searched blindly for you.
You were nowhere.
I could not find you.
I touched every hand and face I could see,
looking for the one I knew to be mine.
Sifted through broken glass as blood
dripped from my fingers,
hot sun piercing down on my back.

—*You were nowhere.*

Somehow vanished from this life we made.
The days were hot and dry as I searched
for the other part of me,
the part that fit right here.

    —Where did you go?

Vanished into the mountains—
under the cover of the stars and the moon,
as you begged for reprieve,
from the skin you did not have.

   —The feelings of the feelings that were just too much.

With scribbled notes and with shaky hands
searching for you,
as we wept.
The first time I lied to you,
not knowing what else to do,
I was scared the world would lose you forever.

I betrayed you
to save you.

The next time,

I solemnly replied *"no."*

Head down, cherry eyes,

I could not bear to read the messages I knew would be sent.

But hours passed,

and they could not find you,

deep in the col,

alone.

If you have any last words of love, you should send them now.

We cannot find them.

We will bring a plane out in the morning.

What are they wearing?

I handed over the photo of us countless times—
at the top of Shepherd Ridge—
you in your black pants and grey shirt,
black shoes.
Your face burned in my memory.
We had no idea when that photograph was taken four weeks prior
the ways in which life would change.

   —*I was too late.*

I held on to you so tightly.
My knuckles white.
Believing I was the salve—
that if I loved you harder you would return, healed.

I simply melted through your fists.

With a seeming refusal to look inward, we blamed each other,
fears and insecurities projected,
as bright and loud as a drive-in movie.

I learned to hate myself,
to shame the places within,
the places that were traumatized,
hurt,
alone.

 —I became the conductor of the train that crashed.

Your words began to haunt me and held me captive.
I had tried to leave but you asked me to stay.

   —*So, I did.*

I stayed.

I had loved you too fiercely to let you walk this path alone,
and even as the walls of our home dissolved around me,
and as your cries echoed in my ears,
fear consuming my entire being,
I stayed.

I held your hand while being stabbed in the back.

    —*It took months for me to bleed out.*

I knew you loved me,
that your actions were borne from your own pain.
The darkness.

I immersed myself in compassion for your experience,
rationalizing it all.
Found understanding in the caves of empathy.

Still, many nights I asked myself, did you mean it?

In this twisted love affair with twisted words,
where up means left and red means square—
I can never seem to figure out what it is you say.
I stay anyhow.
I allow my words to be disassembled,
strung into a word play.
I allowed for you to tell me that what I meant
was something different than what sat in my heart.

    —Too scared to let go.

For 349 days,
you laid flat
on your back.
Unable to see the
sun in your reflection,
the promise in your breath.

—*The gift of a new day.*

You left you and came back them.

Forced to grieve the loss of the person I fell in love with
while learning from scratch this new person
who came wounded and bandaged,
battered and broken.

I made it my life's work to love you properly, the way you
deserved.

To take what was here rather than what was lost,
grateful that you were here at all.

Learning from you, how to give in love.

—*When is giving too much?*

But over time your anger and resentment for me
grew—
an overgrown ivy,
suffocating the musty oak panels
of the old, worn-out cabin
of our love.

    —I became the enemy.

Many nights I needed you.
Many nights I fell asleep crying,
eyes slowly dropping
like a baby after a long cry,
after they had been scooped up and loved,
when they could finally
breathe.

I would like to remind you
that you did not scoop me up.
You did not offer me reprieve.
I simply fell into a slumber
on clouds of grief as I lay
somberly
holding myself
in arms I wished were yours.

And it messed with my head,
that one day you loved me,
and the next you hated me.

Propped me up on a pedestal,
only to knock me down.
I never knew where I stood,
unsure footing
in the air or on the ground,
spinning but never stopping,
on this merry-go-round.

You used to provide shade on sunny days
and warmth when it was too cold.
Your love saved me from my grief
when I was too weak to stand.
But now your love is nowhere to be found,
and it hits me where it saved me until I hit the ground.

I tried to share the empty rooms of my heart with you,
but you were on the attack.

    —always on attack.

You did not see the battles I fought while you dreamed.
You could not hear the pain ringing in my ears,
the fierce ripping at my heart,
sweat piercing my eyes—
the gritty grinding of my teeth—
you were not there while I wept in bed.

Slowly,
my guards went up.

Rusted out armour and shaky knees,
a body ready to sleep 300 lifetimes,
my mind weak and heavy.
It is easy to miss what happens under the bright white stars,
in dark bedrooms,
in the quiet of night.
No fault of your own when you are fast asleep,
but know, that while you dreamt in your olive and navy
bamboo sheets,
I was in a waking nightmare.

>   —*It was not lost on me that you were fighting your own
>   battle.*

I wanted to feel the love again,
I wanted to feel the light.

It felt serene to be loved by you.
But the truth is,
if I can be honest—
I had not felt your warm love wrapped around me
since the icy grass was flattened out from the last heavy
snow fall.

Your words bit
like the Inland Taipan.
My silent acceptance was my flaw.
I should have spoken my mind,
been honest,
told you that you felt sticky,
and hard.

    —Yet I held on to you like a lifeline.

My mind sat captive,
fed words I knew not to be truth,
believing them anyhow.

Because, if I deserved better,
why did you not treat me that way?

I could not let go,
even when I wanted freedom.
My love for you held me hostage.

Too scared to leave,
too pained to stay.

Alone on Christmas Island.
You circled in a life raft forever
while I lay with the crabs,
tell me I deserve it.

Where was my hammock
to avoid the incessant claws for one night.

   —*Nowhere.*

You never knew how lucky you were
to have a life raft and the ability to paddle away.

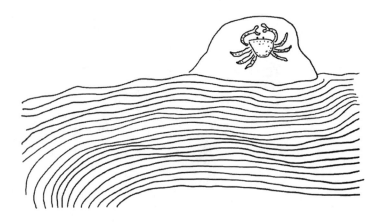

I laid down on my island of crabs as they devoured me.

I blamed myself for a long time.

When you called me selfish, I felt like you did not really know what that word meant.

Selfish was holding on to me because you wanted my heart, even when you mistreated it.

Yet—

when you loved me, your love felt like the ocean where we met.
Deep,
vast,
mysterious,
full of possibilities.

I had forgotten the strength of the ocean.
as quickly as it sucks you in,
it can spit you out.
Toss you around in the sand,
crashing against the rocks with such force
that you wake up alone, strung out against the shore,
not knowing where you are—
only that you do not recognize this place.

It is empty,
it is cold.
There is fear here.
The water is murky, and it smells of death.
Skeletons of our past engulf our sense of present
and so, I am held in the graves
of these great white bellies
where I will be tossed around, blindly.

On a sunny day you would spit me out,
blindly forgetting the day before,
and I would lay dazed and confused,
but only for a moment before I was expected
to find the first aid kit to bandage up any wounds
we endured the day before.

—*I am the patient and the caregiver.*

Sometimes I forget
all the wars you started.

Your bids kept taking from me
my greatest love,
and I would like to say to you—
that it hurt.

You told me once to say these words
When my heart lay bare, open on the floor.

My darling, hold me.

    —My darling, hold me.

My body felt a pain and anguish
it had not felt before.

—*A death I could not grieve.*

What now?

You were my forever.

Your absence a finality I refused to accept.

With it came an insurmountable
amount of trauma
that I never could really shake.

I wanted us back,

I wanted you back,

in the same pieces before we fell apart.

> —*It took me a long time to realize I was asking for the impossible.*

The Summit

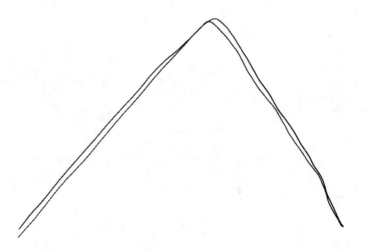

My aching heart waited on forever for you to come back to me.

She said, "you've experienced a lot of losses,"
as I looked down and wept,
could not bring myself to show my face,
and the years of regret.
"The past tends to show itself in the present,
what they say is true -
and I would be willing to bet
the love you are giving now
is to prevent any more loves lost to you."

The trauma soon engulfed me,
a flame within my soul.
The empty space beside me mocked
the you-shaped hole
inside.

Sleep became elusive,
the captive who could not be kept.
My mind ran restless,
a nightmare vivid on daylight hills.
Grief held me underwater,
tied chains to my wrists,
and threw me overboard.

Waves crashed along the fault line,
smooth clear pink skies—
the loud lapping green tide pulled me under.

Calm.

Sometimes chaos is
the familiar, unwelcome
house guest
you wish would remove their shoes
and talk a little quieter.

Still, I watched out the window like that night in October.

The streets bare,
you were nowhere.

I remember the first time you bayed—
"Rip off the bandage."

All I am—
Fabric and gauze held together with glue.
All that is piecing us together.
One pull and I am gone.
Wash off the gray stick collected in the corners,
your pink skin will calm,
and you will be gone,
while I lay with the tissues that once dried our tears,
rather than on the warm arm I thought I was attached to
in a more meaningful way
than glue.

I did not know I was a bandage,
that my job was to hold together
old wounds,
to stop the bleeding.

I thought I was warm coffee
comforting you as you woke to each wintry morning.
The wide-open ocean,
showing you every possibility life had to offer after heartbreak.
I thought I was a bed covered with soft, plush, lavender pillows and comforters, ready to hold you and show you what love really felt like.
The light that made your smile curl from temple bone to temple bone,
so wide I thought your face might break.
I thought I was the hot fire after a chilly day,
the sand between your toes,
the sun beating down on your back.
I thought my love was more
than a bandage.

But that is what a bandage does,

it closes those wounds that do not heal and makes them invisible to the eye.

Perhaps my hand allowed you to live life,

sipping coffee, playing on beaches,

wrapped in warm beds by fireplaces, laughing with your head back.

But the wound would not heal because it needed more.

So, I am now discarded

as a piece of fabric, gauze, and glue,

the only thing holding together me and you.

My mind became the black sky
the night you asked for my hand.

There were no warning bells before our hurricane,
no time to evacuate or board up the windows.
No last words of love before the storm.
The windows crashed in, and the water surged—
everything afloat and nothing to hold on to,
the details of our precious life,

drowning,
drowning.

I held on to my belief that we could make it through,
I grabbed hold of my faith in you—
in your love for me.
But it could not withstand my weight
and kept pulling me under.
My grief,
my pain.
Your love turned into the storm that left me
stranded on the beach,
clothes torn,
skin lashed and cut,
eyes burning from the salt.

My life in ruins around me.
Where do I begin—
how do I pick up these pieces?
How do I put this puzzle together again?
You lit up my life and provided me safety
when no one else would,
the way no one else could,
and without warning it was ripped from me.

That night you left without a trace,
I watched out our bay window for hours—
thirty-six to be exact.
Your tire wells never rolled up,
no familiar beep of the key fob,
I never saw your face.

I felt like such a fool
as I sat there defending you.

Our family now on either side of a string can.

Diagnoses fall discarded by complacency for them,

tirelessly blaming others for the chemistry in our brains.

Our past lives,

the titanic as it sunk.

You told me I saved you,

I was the life raft,

I gave you fresh air when you could not breathe,

warm clothes when you lay bare,

my touch was the touch you had been waiting for your whole life.

But—

I see now the iceberg.

What is under the surface is as expansive

as the entire ocean,

as cold as the arctic circle.

One hit caused the crack that engulfed our whole lives.

Many nights I cried for the little girl inside,
as she died.
She died
a million times.

Every time you left,
and each time you stayed,
as you beat her with words borne from your own insecurities.

She did not know how to love you,
and she did not know how to let go,

So, she laid in her crab torn hammock,
dirt and tear-stained cheeks—
still,
stagnant,
waiting,
praying.

Packed our life into 93 cardboard boxes.
Sorted through scattered dreams
and broken promises,
misplaced timing,
unrequited love,
resentment,
anger.

And moved,
alone.

My things and yours,
without you.

You slept on my faded-out, peach, queen blow-up mattress
on the floor of my cousin's apartment for thirteen months.

Most days were silence as you worked to rebuild your life,
my only peace knowing you were safe in that makeshift bed.

Many nights I sat bargaining with fate,
praying for things to change,
to somehow be different,
better,
back to normal.

   —*Ignorantly dismissing your experience with each plea
   for you to get better.*

I grasped at everything available to save,
salvage, trade, and pillage for our days of deep,
intense love.

> —*You were right when you said there had been too much*
> *destruction here.*

Then, one sunny January morning you emerged,
light as the breeze on the curtains where we shared our first
kiss—
airy—
the seasons had shifted
and so had we.
We rekindled our fire
and held our hands close to keep warm.

But it was always a matter of bad timing.

The Descent

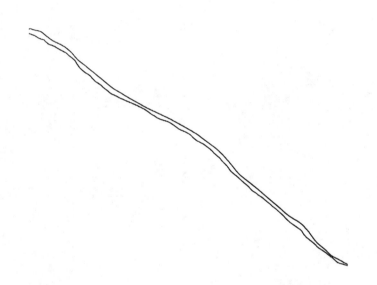

All those months I had sat idly by,
loving you,
as you focused on your own healing.

I want to remind you
that I loved you,
and my love was not weak.
It was strong,
like the rock in the river,
rooted,
as the grand oak tree
where we sat playing cards.

You came back
different.
Weathered.
Worn.
Angry,
and full of resentments.
You were not the
you I had known before.
Your face I did not recognize.

   —*But still, I loved you anyhow.*

I wanted to learn to love
in the ways you needed me to.
I gave my heart like a swallow gives song
to a new dawn breaking.
A waterfall crashing down,
I poured my love in to learning how
to do it better.

When you needed space
I would remind myself
it was not selfish
and it was not to hurt me,
it was a need of yours.

To think,
and to come back to yourself.

With time you would find calm
and be ready to talk.

   —*I had hoped for so much but reminded myself, it was
   not about me.*

This was your journey.
I loved you more
than my best laid plans for us
and so, I supported you
to take your space.

—Even when it was killing me inside.

I had promised to always
come to you,
to run my fingers
through your hair,
hold your face,
and kiss
your forehead.

And although I may hurt you,
and I would,
for I am human—
I would try not to,
because your heart was precious to me,
and so was being trusted with it.

Our love
was precious
and rare.
It was not to be taken for granted,
yet in those early years
you felt I took it for granted.

    —For that, I would like to say I am sorry.

I held hope.
Hope that we would hold space for one another
and eventually
find peace with each other.

     —Like it was the only thing I knew how to hold on to.

I wanted to remember what it felt like to be loved by you,
the nights you read me to sleep
wrapped in your arms.
The nights I thought you did not know how to let me go.

I begged to wake from this nightmare,
but,
the sun refused to come up.
Perpetual state of darkness,
cloud cover held us hostage.
No stars to connect,
no blurred ombre mix of orange, red, and purple
as the backdrop of our love.

I imagine you looked up to those cloud covered stars overhead
as you stepped out on to those kelp-covered rocks
that crisp April night.

The beach we picnicked at last summer—
climbed into your life raft and, oak-oar in hand, pulled away.

Paddled off into the dark, moonlit currents of
love-starved sirens hiding within the circling driftwood below.

Beneath the tide, droplets of water seeped through the frayed seal of the sky light above,

waking me from my last sleep paralyzed by the fear of losing you.

    —You were gone.

Impermanence life's only promise.

I broke in to a million pieces that night
and never fit back together again
in the same way.

Our love story was quick,
it was fleeting,
you left as quickly as you came,
and I desired to remember you.

I desired to remember that you loved me
purely during our time together.
That you held me tightly,
like you did not know how to let go.

So, I sat still, and I remembered
how it felt to be held by you.

I remembered the warm words you whispered
over my shoulder as we stood at the kitchen sink.

Overcome by the visceral knowing that—
until the day you reached out your hands to me again,
I would miss you,
and my weary heart would beat a little bit slower,
for it had lost a part of itself.

Your silence,
an old, weathered house.
Empty,
dark,
save for the crunching of memories
strewn on the dirty, soil covered floor
was our bed each night.

The grief was unapologetic.

It held me in a paralytic loop of our love and memories trapped in a tungsten box.

I watched silently as grief crept in, fluffed a pillow and laid down,
the superfluous blow-in I did not know I needed.

It permeated, opened each cell in my body and took up residence,
Invited, no—
forced me to feel the ubiquitous hold it had on me.

As it did, I listened.

The loss of you taught me the fragility of life,
to give in love freely—
because someone you love today
may not be here tomorrow.

The cavernous depths of my grief were relative to the highs of my joy—

a testament to our summits.

And, the mundane brought with it an unexpected peace.

   —*In laying in thick despair, even the mundane becomes sanctuary.*

Your love taught me how to love deeply,
cracked open my tender heart,
and showed me the intricacies of sorrow and empathy.

You taught me how to listen to understand,
to release my ego in exchange for care,
gifting myself permission to open to love.

In-parallel, our experiences reintroduced me to the love I
had for myself,
taught me how to practice the word *no*—
to establish boundaries in protection of my own well-being.

   —*Boundaries keep the peace in.*

I sunk into the strength of my resolve to learn and to grow,

Broke open by the forced acceptance that sometimes in love we must set free those we wish to hold close.

I learned to love you from afar, grateful to know you existed at all.

My grief became a part of me,
and life's meaning began to echo in those daylight hills
as I grew quiet,
and learned to listen.

Acknowledging that losing in love does not equate to losing love, and perhaps it is not a loss at all.

Our growth felt by those we have yet to love.

Give in love—

releasing expectations while accepting that relationships are nuanced.

Give in love—

exchanging judgements for curiosity.

Give in love—

for what you focus on will shine brightly back on to you.

To give in love is a choice we make every moment of every day,

the result of which is all that truly lives on after our death.

—Love holds the liminal between birth and rebirth.

Your love is everywhere.

You are the smell of rhubarb crumble,

the wind that runs its fingers through my hair.

You are the prose deliberately strung together on tear-stained, dog-eared pages of devoured books,

the streetlights lighting my way home.

You are the hot sand beneath my feet,

and each chord of the songs that will forever play as the soundtrack to our love.

You are every raven high in the sky,

and when I miss you, I look up

and watch you fly.

When times are difficult,
I would like you to remember
that the wind is at your back.
Fly south.

When you are weary,
come sit on my branches awhile.

Tepid water lapped at my feet as my toes sunk in to the warm, wet sand that muggy August sunset.

I placed four daisies in the tide as you flew off towards the horizon.
White petals danced in and out with the calm waves as forgiveness caught my reflection.

One for our peak,
our ridge,
our summit,
and our descent.

    —An ocean of love unwasted.

I cannot remember your laugh lines now,
or the way our fingers laced together.

That scar on the left side of your right index finger is but a
distant memory.

But when I use my white foam hand soap I will smile,
and only you know why.

My umbrella always had room for two,
and I would have loved you forever.